February 22,

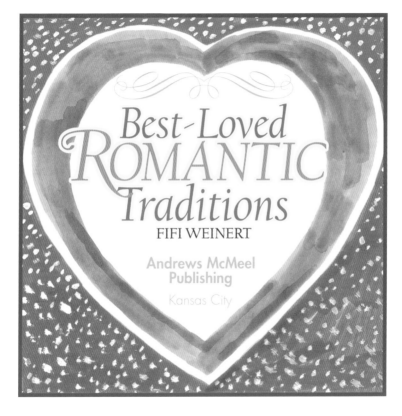

Best-Loved
ROMANTIC
Traditions

FIFI WEINERT

Andrews McMeel
Publishing

Kansas City

ISBN: 0-7407-1027-3

Library of Congress Catalog Card Number: 00-102165

To protect the privacy of all who contributed to this project, no signature or photograph has any connection with its proximate text. What joins text, signatures, and images together is their unified spirit of love.

Special thanks to Sabrina Henley and Lisa Martin.

To my favorite romantics, Caspar and Janet.

Contents

$\mathcal{T}$his book is a collection of private romantic traditions. We think of traditions as precious rituals or heirlooms passed from generation to generation. But these traditions are different. They grow out of one couple's history. They are not meant to endure beyond the love that brought them into being. They are personal celebrations of romance. We hope these celebrations, and the poems and love letters interspersed between them, add to the celebration of your romance. Surely they express the best loved of all romantic traditions—love itself.

—F. W. '99

Ours Alone

"Our song" that we only
dance to with each other.

Our wedding vows
repeated once a decade.

10 Best-Loved Romantic Traditions

$\mathcal{M}$any couples have
traditions that start and
end with their own romance.

I met my husband on a park bench that faces two almost-touching trees.
We call them our "lover trees." On our anniversary, we join our trees
together with crepe-paper ribbons and eat lunch on our park bench sharing
the company of our devoted counterparts.

—Joyce (Mrs. Austin) Jones

On every one of our wedding anniversaries I bake a heart-shaped straw-berry shortcake with as many layers as years my husband Ralph and I have been together. Now that we've passed the six-year mark, some of my cakes look like a pyramid and some look like the Leaning Tower of Pisa. But nobody cares. As long as Ralph, our three little ones, and I keep adding layers, we're happy with any cake I bake.

—Susan Rifkin (married to Ralph Levey)

The favorite romance in my family was between my grandmother, Virginia Thayer, and her husband, Grandpa M. Supposedly, every day they were together he gave her a red rose.

When Joe and I got married, I made him promise that in memory of Grandma V's and Popsi's love, he'd keep up their rose tradition.

He did. But on my first birthday as a bride, he came home empty-handed. Just before I got upset, he led me to our bedroom. While I'd been at work he'd returned to our apartment and sprinkled rose petals over the carpet, pillowcases, and sheets.

The next day I gathered the petals together and put them in a potpourri bowl with hopes Joe would soon repeat his wonderful surprise.

—Marsha (Mrs. Joe) Rapaport

My love and my darling,

It is ten minutes past eight. I must tell you how much I love you at ten minutes past eight on a Sunday evening, January 27th, 1918 . . .

My love for you tonight is so deep and tender that it seems to be outside myself as well. I am fast shut up like a little lake in the embrace of some big mountains, you would see me down below, deep and shining—and quite fathomless, my dear. You might drop your heart into me and you'd never hear it touch bottom. I love you—I love you— Goodnight.

Oh, Bogey, what it is to love like this!

—Katherine Mansfield to
John Middleton Murry

Roger and I were high-school sweethearts who separated before we went to college. Yet I immediately recognized his voice when he unexpectedly phoned me thirty-five years later. We were both divorced.

"Why don't I fly out to San Francisco and see you?" he suggested. I thought he was insane.

But when I saw him, the years vanished. We spent our first month together exploring California and each other.

Then it struck us—we both had grown children. How were they going to feel about our newly rekindled romance?

They soon answered our question for us. When Roger and I decided to permanently live together, they presented us with two stars purchased from the International Star Registry.

Their gift was accompanied by a note which read, "May you two always shine together. Love, your five favorite meteorites—Susan, Seth, Ralph, Charles, and Liza."

—Gail Hepper (married to Roger Millichet)

(You can call the Star Registry at [800] 283-3333)

Love's Language

*O*ur exposure to romance begins with childhood fairy tales in which the gallant prince wins the heart of the beautiful princess and carries her off to live happily ever after.

We later learn there are songs of romance, popular show tunes, opera arias, and ballads that express the feelings of romance when those feelings are not poetically thought of as a song.

A Tabu perfume advertisement from the 1960s stood framed by my Aunt Melissa's bed. It showed a woman being swept away from her piano playing by a dark, handsome man.

"That's my story," Aunt Melissa confided while we were having tea. "Your Uncle Harry was my piano teacher. Sometimes after my lessons we would sing Lieder together. As I sang I would watch his powerful hands running down the keys. One day as we were singing, he bent over and kissed me. We already were in love!

"As soon as I saw this picture I cut it out of the magazine and framed it. Your uncle bought me my first bottle of the perfume.

"Harry was always my passion," she continued. "And Tabu is the only perfume that I wear."

—Stella Bracken

Dearest—

I wish I had the gift of making rhymes, for methinks there is poetry in my head and heart since I have been in love with you. You are a Poem. Of what sort, then? Epic? Mercy on me, no! A sonnet? No; for that is too labored and artificial. You are a sort of sweet, simple, gay, pathetic ballad, which Nature is singing, sometimes with tears, sometimes with smiles, and sometimes with intermingled smiles and tears.

—Nathaniel Hawthorne to Sophia Hawthorne
December 5, 1839

$\mathcal{T}$here are dances of romance—
the waltz, the flamenco, and the
gracefully seductive tango.

I was fifteen. In modern dance class I twisted my knee, broke my kneecap, and trapped shards of bone in my knee joint. Would I ever dance again?

My surgeon assured me I would. He bought me a music box with a twirling ballerina. "You must save the first dance for me," he insisted. I promised that I would. But when the music box broke, I felt it was an omen. "Ridiculous," he said.

A few days later I woke up in my hospital bed and discovered my music box was magically working once again. That morning I took my first excruciating postoperative steps.

Dr. Jordan waited six years—until my wedding—to confess he'd exchanged my broken music box for one that worked. Before dancing with my husband or my father, I'd saved the first dance for him as I still do in my memory whenever I dance at a happy event in my life.

—Rita (Mrs. Ralph) Chaldic

And there are foods of romance offered as enticements of love.

My husband knows that I love chocolate. I also love his kisses. Whenever he goes on a business trip, he hides foil-covered chocolate kisses in places I'm likely to find them—coat pockets, dresser drawers, even shoes.

Sometimes there are notes with these hidden confections. "I'm kissing your fingers, your shoulders, your toes." Lately I've started to write back. I bury kisses in his suitcase, each wrapped in paper that asks, "Where would you like me to kiss you now?"

—Suki (Mrs. Carl) Stone

$\mathcal{T}$here is also a vast secret language
of romance in which the placement of
stamps conveys romantic meaning . . .

*In high school we often sent our crushes letters in stamp-coded
envelopes. An upside down stamp in the upper right-hand corner
of an envelope meant* I LOVE YOU, *in the lower right-hand corner*
LOTS OF KISSES, *in the lower left-hand corner* LET'S GO STEADY, *and
in the upper left-hand corner* MEET ME TONIGHT.

—Brenda Shamis

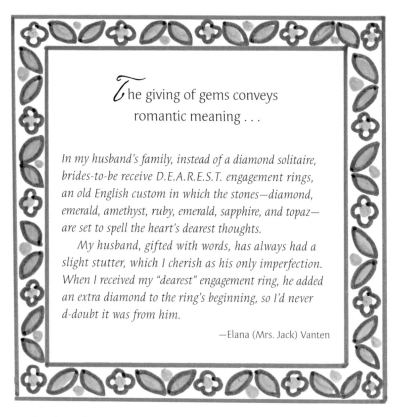

*T*he giving of gems conveys
romantic meaning . . .

*In my husband's family, instead of a diamond solitaire,
brides-to-be receive D.E.A.R.E.S.T. engagement rings,
an old English custom in which the stones—diamond,
emerald, amethyst, ruby, emerald, sapphire, and topaz—
are set to spell the heart's dearest thoughts.*

*My husband, gifted with words, has always had a
slight stutter, which I cherish as his only imperfection.
When I received my "dearest" engagement ring, he added
an extra diamond to the ring's beginning, so I'd never
d-doubt it was from him.*

—Elana (Mrs. Jack) Vanten

A famous playwright once handed his wife a bag of peanuts. "I wish they were emeralds," he exclaimed. Our story was the reverse. At our engagement Peter presented me with a large emerald ring inscribed "D.G. Thank you for Springtime."

Years later, the ring was stolen. "Let me replace it," Peter said. "I'd rather have peanuts," I suggested. We used the insurance money to fund a park.

On the day the park opened a crate of peanuts arrived at our front door with a note that said, "The season of our love never changes. Peter." We've now funded seven other parks. Peter always sends me the same crate of peanuts and the same reminder. We both found Springtime when we found each other.

—Constance "Dear" Green-Coglin

And flowers act as messages of love.

I felt betrayed when Bill died. He'd promised to outlive me. This wasn't fair. On my birthday I could hardly get out of bed. Then the doorbell rang. I thought, "No doubt another cruel mistake." On all of my birthdays during our marriage, Bill had sent me a bouquet of orange blossoms to remind me I was still his "bride." There was my familiar bouquet and a note: "Although you do not know this, we are never far apart. I'm the angel on your shoulder. I'm the love inside your heart. Let these flowers reassure you that my thoughts are with you still. You are my bride forever, and I'll always be your Bill. Please continue living for both of us."

When I phoned the florist, I learned that after his first heart attack, Bill had arranged to have flowers sent on all my future birthdays and had written years and years of notes. Of course I wept, and then decided that for both of us I had to continue life.

—Leila (Mrs. Bill) Rogers

As if all this were not enough, we even have a holiday of romance: Valentine's Day, February 14.

Before there were Valentine's Day cards, there were love postcards and packets of love notes. "Love notes," promissory pledges of sweet intentions brought from the imaginary Bank of True Love, still make splendid gifts for lovers—even if, like some New Year's resolutions, their promises are not kept.

When Alan and I were dating, we always made love on the leather couch in my parents' den. When my parents moved to New Mexico several years ago, they were going to give "our" couch to the Salvation Army. Fortunately, we salvaged it just in time and put it in Alan's office.

That year we made a Valentine's promise to one another. One day a month we'd meet for a "sweetheart date"—a date on which we'd pretend we were still courting.

On the second Wednesday of almost every month (we had our first date on a Wednesday), we meet in the city, have dinner together, take a walk, buy a bottle of inexpensive wine, and end the evening on our couch of memories—kissing for several uninterrupted hours before going home to our "real" life.

—Stephanie (Mrs. Alan) Moser

Every Valentine's our friends and family share a red and white dinner party. Half the fun is inventing table decorations—red candles set in radish roses, salt and red pepper in mushroom caps, a centerpiece of red tulips in a sugar-stenciled canning jar. The other half is planning the menu. We've tried beet soup and sour cream, tomatoes and mozzarella, corned beef and mashed potatoes, meringues with raspberry sherbet, and strawberries in white wine. Of course, not in one meal! We want the Valentine's spirit to continue long after the party ends. It always does.

—Raing and Arthur Lastien

$\mathcal{B}$ut while our lives are filled
with the diversions of romance,
what is romance? Romance is
a special kind of love.

What Is Romance?

$\mathcal{R}$omance is what the poet W. B. Yeats once called "the old highway of love." It is the love that starts with surprised discovery, leads to sensual intoxication and wild generosity, and ends with happily ever after. It is the love that crosses all boundaries and follows the sweetest impulses of the heart.

Quatrain

What is this day with two suns in the sky?

Day unlike other days,

with a great voice giving it to the planet,

Here it is, enamored beings, your day!

—Jalāl ad-Dīn Rūmī, 1207–1273

My husband, Steven, disappeared for several hours while skiing in Colorado. I was frantic, especially when by nightfall he still had not been found. Fortunately, the ski patrol discovered him the next morning with a bit of frostbite and a broken shoulder. My initial terror quickly turned to anger—he'd been skiing on an especially steep mountain. Then I experienced relief. Thank God that he wasn't hurt badly.

From that day on, Steven and I started a tradition of praying together every morning at the very hour he was found—8:30 Mountain time. As we work together, we usually pray at home before we leave for our office. But if we're apart for any reason, we place a call to each other and just share a moment of gratitude for our continued lives.

—Selma (Mrs. Steven) Ban

*T*he Western ideal of romance first took shape in the fourteenth-century French court, when knights championed ladies by undertaking dangerous, often time-consuming quests. Although Ralph Waldo Emerson suggests "give all to love," traditionally, romance is courageous but never reckless. It follows a gently familiar pattern.

From Unending Love

I seem to have loved you in numberless forms,
numberless times.
In life after life, in age after age forever.
My spell-bound heart has made and re-made the
necklace of songs.
That you take as a gift, wear round your neck
in your many forms
In life after life, in age after age forever.

—Sir Rabindranath Tagore, 1861–1941
Translated by William Radice, 1983

*R*omance usually begins
with a *coup de foudre*—
a lightning bolt of
lovers' recognition.

My family is filled with stories of love at first sight. My mother and
father were married within six weeks of their first official date.

I did not expect to follow in their footsteps. Then I met Seth.

I was a real estate broker representing an apartment he wanted to look
at. We met in the lobby. "You have a glow around you," he told me.
"You're my Beatrice." "How did you know my name was Beatrice?" I asked
him. "I didn't," he answered. "I was thinking of Beatrice in Dante's
Paradiso. You're my Beatrice leading me to heaven."

I was really leading him to the two-bedroom apartment we now live in.
Seth still claims he sees a glow whenever he looks at me. I guess he does.

To keep up appearances, I like to illuminate our bedroom with softly
glowing candles so he can see me in my best light.

—Beatrice (Mrs. Seth) Krebbs

*W*hy do lovers experience
immediate recognition?
According to romantic tradition,
lovers are seen as two parts of
a long ago separated whole.

*I*n Plato's *Symposium* the myth of this separation is told through the playwright Aristophanes. Originally all human beings were doubles—with double faces, limbs, and organs. Zeus, annoyed by human arrogance, divided these double creatures and condemned them to seek their missing halves throughout eternity. True love occurs when we find our perfect match.

If lovers do not recognize each other at first sight, they surely do at first kiss.

The soul-expanding sensory
awakening of love's first
rapturous embrace, this exchange
of life breath, is frequently
portrayed as a physical merging
that blurs identities.

I Want to Breathe

you in I'm not talking about
Perfume or even the sweet o-

Dour of your skin but the
air itself. I want to share

Your air inhaling what you
Exhale I'd like to be that

close two of us breathing
each other as one as that.

—James Laughlin, b. 1914

*H*owever passionately as lovers may seem to merge in their first embrace, romantic love traditionally remains chaste until sanctified by commitment. It is not a physical desire that must be consummated. Rather it is a spiritual force that elevates us to our best selves. It returns us to innocence so that we kiss and the angels sing the sweetest songs we've ever heard.

Shortly after we got married, my precious Felicia was diagnosed with lymphoma. She went through a year of chemotherapy in which her survival hung in the balance. But somehow during even the worst moments of treatment hearing music calmed her mind, especially the great opera arias.

When she miraculously recovered, I decided to surprise her with a special opera—an outdoor presentation of Aida *in Carnac. During the first intermission she began to cry. "All the time I was sick," she told me, "I dreamed I was holding you under the stars as angels sang to us—they promised me we'd have a life together."*

"And we do," I said. We have been married fourteen years and spend every anniversary at the opera with the singing angels we both hear.

—George Romez

The Gifts of Romance

The spiritual elevation
of romantic love encourages
us to give completely of
our own resources.

We never had the money for a vacation home so my husband, a gifted artist, painted my dreams—cottages and castles. Whenever he got a raise, I got another beautiful house to hang on our bedroom wall.

Until this year, when he handed me a deed to our land in Vermont and asked me to pick my favorite painting. "That's the home we'll build," he said. With all the incredible homes he's helped me to envision, I don't know how to choose. As a tribute to his imagination, I've given the choice to him.

—Vita (Mrs. Colin) Sutter

It is never the cost of a lover's gift but its intent that makes it valuable. We all remember O. Henry's Christmas story, "The Gift of the Magi," in which a poor but adoring wife sells her hair to buy a gold watch for her husband's treasured pocket watch. Ironically—and yes, romantically— she discovers that he has sold his watch to buy combs for her glorious long hair.

My husband is a heart researcher. His first gift to me was a set of heart-shaped buttons I sewed on a cardigan I still wear. On every occasion, we exchange heart-shaped gifts. Our collection now ranges from a Jim Dine lithograph to a Baccarat green crystal heart, to a heart-shaped willow wreath that hangs on our front door—promising a loving welcome to all our guests.

—Margo (Mrs. Ralph) Kettinger

The Promises of Romance

*B*ut even more precious than
the gifts of romance are its promises.
Romance assures us of who we are.

When I told my mom I wanted to be an artist she was furious. "Who do
you think you are?" she asked. "The queen of art?" I was heartsick my
family didn't share my dreams.

But my boyfriend, Alfred, did. We'd been planning to eventually get
married. "Marry me now," he said, "We'll move to New York and I'll
support you while you start your career."

To save money I cooked so many chicken liver dinners in our fourth-
floor walkup I thought of writing a chicken liver cookbook.

I slowly began to show my collages. Eventually I became successful
enough to support Alfred through law school.

Last month at our annual New Year's party, as we put on our foil
crowns and blew our noisemakers, I remembered my mother's words. Now
I am the Queen of Art but my husband has always been the King of Love.

—Sophia (Mrs. Alfred) Kates

Our friends and family tell us that we're crazy. While most couples share an apartment, Malachi and I do not. We've been together for eight years. We both are writers and we both like our space.

Three weeks of one month I stay at his apartment, three weeks of the next month he stays at mine. One week of every month we live separately.

Our monthly separations give us the chance to rediscover one another. When we're apart we anticipate our reunions; we remember the reasons we love each other; and we have the chance to reinvent ourselves. We find absence and abstinence make the heart grow fonder. At least they do for us.

—Ruth (Mrs. Malachi) File

*R*omance assures us
we are bound
to our soul mate.

Fräulein Felice!

. . . Write to me only once a week, so that your letter arrives on Sunday—for I cannot endure your daily letters, I am incapable of enduring them. For instance, I answer one of your letters, then lie in bed in apparent calm, but my heart beats through my entire body and is conscious only of you. I belong to you; there is really no other way of expressing it, and that is not strong enough. But for this very reason I don't want to know what you are wearing; it confuses me so much that I cannot deal with life; and that's why I don't want to know that you are fond of me. If I did, how could I, fool that I am, go on sitting in my office, or here at home, instead of leaping on to a train with my eyes closed and opening them only when I am with you? . . .

—Franz Kafka to Felice Bauer,
November 11, 1912

And finally, romance guarantees us
that neither time or space will
have dominion over our youth,
our perfection, or the constancy
of our hearts.

My husband, David, and I met in college. I took my junior year in Barcelona. When I unpacked my suitcase upon arrival, I found an envelope containing a Victorian locket and a note.

Inside the locket were two small photographs, one of David, and one of me. "I'm always with you. Love, Your Husband-to-be," the note said.

From then on, passing the locket back and forth between us became our secret tradition. Whenever either of us went on a trip alone, the locket went with the traveler.

Last year at David's funeral, I placed the locket in his casket. The rabbi noticed what I'd done, so I explained our tradition. "This is David's longest trip alone," I said. "I just want him to know I'm with him."

"I'm sure he knows," the rabbi answered, giving me a hug. And for a moment I almost felt David hugging me—assuring me that part of him is still with me.

—Lea (Mrs. David) Mendel

Late Fragment

And did you get what

You wanted from this life, even so?

I did

And what did you want?

To call myself beloved, to feel myself

beloved on the earth

—Raymond Carver, 1938–1988

Photo Credits

Special thanks to the following who submitted photographs:

Jennifer Fox
Erin Friedrich
Christi Clemons Hoffman
JuJu Johnson
Julie Phillips

Text Credits

$\mathcal{I}$f you would like to contribute your traditions to future books, please e-mail us at fifistraditions@aol.com. Future subjects under consideration are baby traditions and mother-daughter traditions.

. . . In our life there is a single color,
as on an artist's palette,
which provides the meaning
of life and art.
It is the color of love.

—Marc Chagall